For Marleigh & Kennedy

ACKNOWLEDGMENT

I would like to thank the following people for their contributions to creating, supporting, maintaining and improving Virtual Visitation facilities in Pennsylvania:
The Honorable Governor Tom Wolf and his predecessor Governor Tom Corbett of Pennsylvania; The Honorable Pennsylvania State Senator Shirley M. Kitchen and the Honorable Pennsylvania State Representative Jake Wheatley, all deserve special mention.

Also, major supporters include: the Honorable John E. Wetzel, Secretary, Pennsylvania Department of Corrections; Cheryl Scott and Keith Fenstermacher, Treatment Programs Administrator, Pennsylvania Department of Corrections and the wardens of the Pennsylvania Department of Corrections and the virtual visitation liaison staffs.

Others deserving of credit include Daniel Stewart, Senior Justice Advisor, Connected Justice Solutions at CISCO Systems, Inc.; Karl Rabke, CISCO Systems, Inc.; Desmond Irving, President, Connection Training Services; Garnett C. Littlepage, Chairman and CEO, Scotlandyard Security Services, Inc.; Susan Neubuck, Virtual Visitation Manager, Scotlandyard Security Services, Inc. and Shanel Hilliard, Executive Director of the Booker T. Washington Center, Erie, PA.

I wish to acknowledge those many unsung contributors to re-entry services such as Dr. Minnie Moore-Johnson and William Hart, Director of Re-Entry Services for the City of Philadelphia, and the many that have dedicated themselves to strengthening families of returning citizens to ensure successful transition to the community through mentoring, education, training, workforce development and supportive services.

I especially appreciate the helpful comments and ideas from the Almost Like Visiting Review Committee, a combination of researchers, experts, caregivers or an adult-child of a formerly incarcerated parent. Thank you Ann Adalist-Estrin, Director, National Resource Center on Children and Families of the Incarcerated, for your support and guidance through the completion of this book.

Shannon Ellis

Almost Like Visiting

Written by: Shannon Ellis

Illustrations by: Katrina Tapper

"Hey Guys!" Jeremiah yells, as he heads to the playground with his sister.

Alex sees his friends,
"Look Ebony, it's Jeremiah and Jordan! Hi!"

Jeremiah shares with excitement, "We just came from seeing our dad. He's so much fun! I love him."

"My dad just took me to get my hair cut. What did you guys do?" Alex asks Jeremiah and Jordan.

"We sat and talked. I told him about school and showed him my list of spelling words."
Says Jeremiah

Jordan tells her friends, "I showed him how I can hula hoop! We saw him on the video."

"Oh, the video on the phone?" Asks Ebony.

Jordan explains to Ebony and Alex, "No, it's on a computer. We go to a special building. My Mom or Grandmom takes us. My dad is far away. We sit in a room with chairs and we can bring toys or anything we want to show our dad!"

"Where is your dad?" Asks Alex.

Jeremiah answers, "He got in trouble and now he is in prison and people are trying to figure out what happened. Almost like timeout except when it happens to grown ups they have to go to prison."

Alex adds to the conversation "Oh Yeah, my mom was in prison because she broke a law and she was gone for two of my birthdays. We never got to see her on the computer. When we did visit my mom it took a really long time to get there but it was great to hug her."

Jeremiah explains, "Not all of us with parents in prison get to see them on the computer, but we all get to see them. We can also go in person. Some-times you can sit in a room with your parent or sit and talk while seeing them through a glass!"

"Do you get to see him a lot?" Asks Ebony.

Jordan replies, "We go to the video visiting build-ing one time a month to see him. Sometimes we see him in person, but it is really far. I love in-person visits but video visiting is a great way to see my Dad in between."

"Video visiting, what's that?" Ebony asks.

"It's like when you can make video calls on the phone or computer!" Jordan explains

Jeremiah explains more, "We go to a building but some people are allowed to see their mom or dad who are in prison from home on a video call."

Ebony asks another question, "Is your dad a bad person?"

Jeremiah continues to explain, "No, he's not a bad person. Mom says sometimes people just make bad choices. Our Dad always tells us to make good choices, to always do what is right and he loves us. I can't wait for him to come home."

"I love my dad. Sometimes it makes us sad and angry that we can't see him or be with him and we cry. Even though I can't go places with him, I am happy he calls me and I can see him in person sometimes. He always makes me laugh and he helps me a lot." Says Jeremiah

Jordan adds, "Yeah! He told me to keep my knees bent when I hula-hoop! But then we had to stop because they let us know our time was almost done. It made me sad, but I'm going to practice for next time. Do you want to see?"

"You are getting good, Jordan. Can you show me how your dad taught you?" Ebony asks Jordan.

Jeremiah interrupts, "Yes, she can show you tomorrow. We need to go inside before the lights come on!"

Alex agrees, "You are right, we all need to be in soon. I liked hearing about the video visiting you can do with your dad. Next time you see him maybe you will be able to tell him you taught Ebony how to hula-hoop using his tips! See ya!"

"Bye!"

94260438R00022

Made in the USA
Middletown, DE
18 October 2018